CHRIS TOMLIN
ARRIVING

ISBN-13: 978-1-4234-2427-7
ISBN-10: 1-4234-2427-1

HAL•LEONARD®
CORPORATION
7777 W. BLUEMOUND RD. P.O. BOX 13819 MILWAUKEE, WI 53213

Visit Hal Leonard Online at
www.halleonard.com

www.christomlin.com

INDESCRIBABLE

Words and Music by LAURA STORY
and JESSE REEVES

Recorded a half step higher.

HOLY IS THE LORD

Words and Music by CHRIS TOMLIN
and LOUIE GIGLIO

HOW GREAT IS OUR GOD

Words and Music by CHRIS TOMLIN,
JESSE REEVES and ED CASH

Recorded a half step lower.

YOUR GRACE IS ENOUGH

Words and Music by
MATT MAHER

Great is ___ Your faith-
Great is ___ Your love _

-ful - ness, ___ oh God. ___
___ and jus - tice, God. ___

God, ___ I see ___ Your ___

for _____ me. ___

UNFAILING LOVE

Words and Music by CHRIS TOMLIN,
ED CASH and CARY PIERCE

THE WAY I WAS MADE

Words and Music by CHRIS TOMLIN,
JESSE REEVES and ED CASH

MIGHTY IS THE POWER OF THE CROSS

Words and Music by SHAWN CRAIG
and CHRIS TOMLIN

*Recorded a half step lower.

is   the   pow - er   of,   might - y   is   the

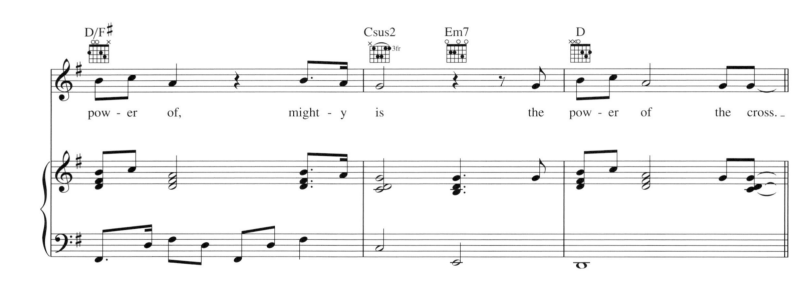

pow - er   of,   might - y   is   the   pow - er   of   the   cross. _

_   Thank   You   for ____   the   cross. _

ALL BOW DOWN

Words and Music by CHRIS TOMLIN
and ED CASH

*Recorded a half step lower.

ON OUR SIDE

Words and Music by CHRIS TOMLIN,
JESSE REEVES and ED CASH

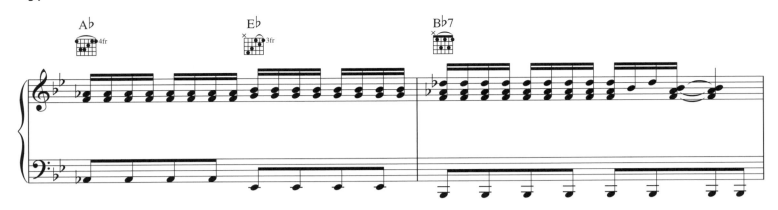

If God is

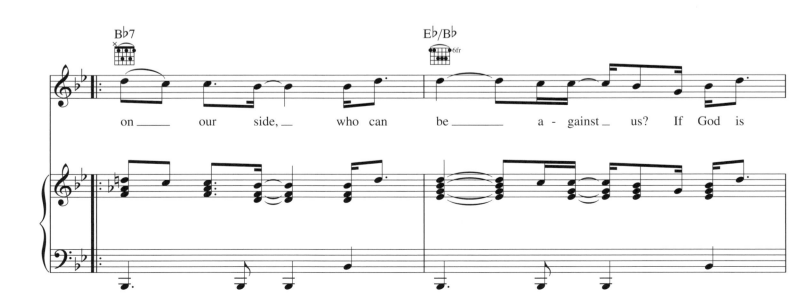

on _____ our side, ___ who can be _____ a - gainst___ us? If God is

on ____ our side, ___ we won't be ____ a - fraid. ____ Though the

moun - tains ___ may fall ___ and the sky will crum - ble, there ain't

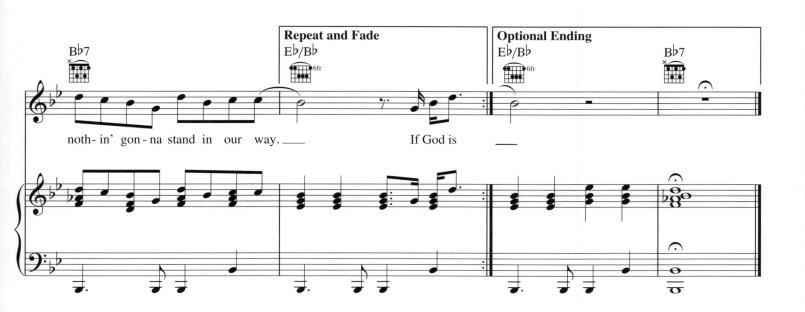

noth- in' gon - na stand in our way. ____ If God is ____

KING OF GLORY

Words and Music by CHRIS TOMLIN
and JESSE REEVES

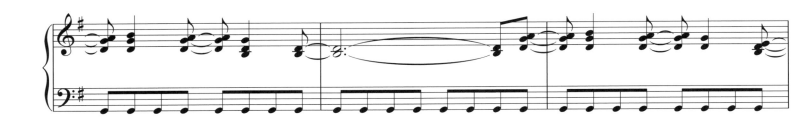

Lift up your gaze, be lift - ed up.
hands, be lift - ed up.

Tell ev - 'ry - one how great _ the love,   the love come
Let the re - deemed de - clare _ the love.   And we bow

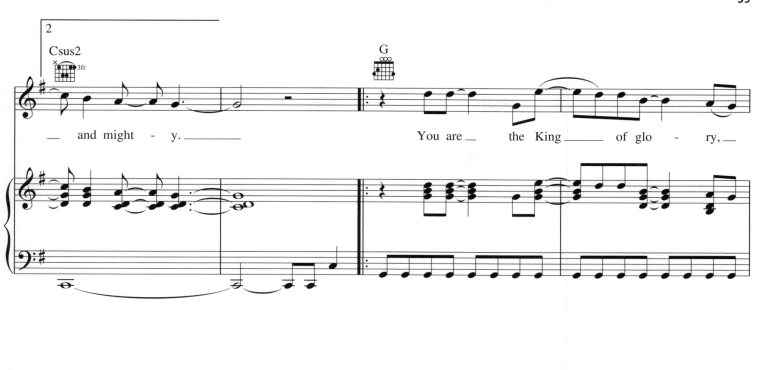

and might - y. ___ You are ___ the King ___ of glo - ry, ___

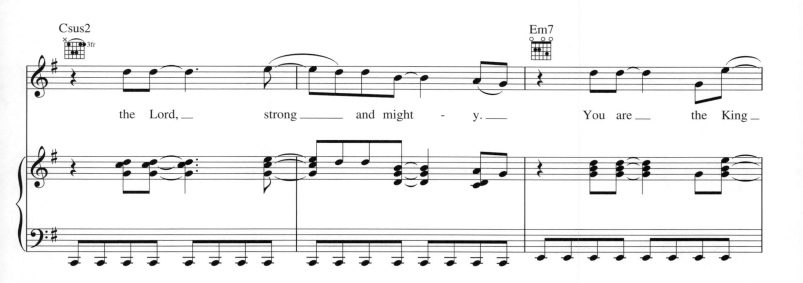

the Lord, ___ strong ___ and might - y. ___ You are ___ the King ___

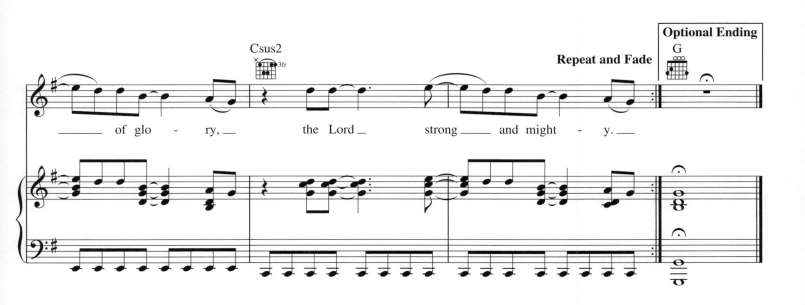

___ of glo - ry, ___ the Lord ___ strong ___ and might - y. ___

Repeat and Fade

Optional Ending

YOU DO ALL THINGS WELL

Words and Music by CHRIS TOMLIN,
JESSE REEVES and MICHAEL JOHN CLEMENT